Marie Antoinette

CHERRY LAKE PRESS

Published in the United States of America by Cherry Lake Publishing Group
Ann Arbor, Michigan
www.cherrylakepublishing.com

Reading Adviser: Beth Walker Gambro, MS, Ed., Reading Consultant, Yorkville, IL
Book Design: Jennifer Wahi
Illustrator: Jeff Bane

Photo Credits: © And-One/Shutterstock, 5; (Attributed to) Johann Georg Weickert, Public domain, via Wikimedia Commons, 7; Unknown author, Public domain, via Wikimedia Commons, 9 and 22; Élisabeth Louise Vigée Le Brun, Public domain, via Wikimedia Commons, 11 and 23; Karl Girardet, Public domain, via Wikimedia Commons, 13; Palace of Versailles, Public domain, via Wikimedia Commons. 15; Jean-Baptiste André Gautier-Dagoty, Public domain, via Wikimedia Commons, 17; Anonymous, Public domain, via Wikimedia Commons, 19; «E. Chavanne», Public domain, via Wikimedia Commons, 21.

Cherry Lake Press is an imprint of Cherry Lake Publishing Group

Library of Congress Cataloging-in-Publication Data

Names: Loh-Hagan, Virginia, author.
Title: Marie Antoinette / written by: Virginia Loh-Hagan.
Description: Ann Arbor, Michigan : Cherry Lake Publishing, [2024] | Series: My itty-bitty bio | Audience: Grades K-1 | Summary: "Many know Marie Antoinette as the last Queen of France, overthrown during the French Revolution, but few know she was also a mother, adopted orphans, and helped the poor and needy. This biography for early readers examines her life in a simple, age-appropriate way that helps young readers develop word recognition and reading skills. This title helps all readers learn about a historical female leader who made a difference in our world. The My Itty-Bitty Bio series celebrates diversity and inclusion, values that readers of all ages can aspire to"-- Provided by publisher.
Identifiers: LCCN 2023035025 | ISBN 9781668937754 (hardcover) | ISBN 9781668938799 (paperback) | ISBN 9781668940136 (ebook) | ISBN 9781668941485 (pdf)
Subjects: LCSH: Marie Antoinette, Queen, consort of Louis XVI, King of France, 1755-1793--Juvenile literature. | Queens--France--Biography--Juvenile literature.
Classification: LCC DC137.1 .L66 2023 | DDC 944/.035092 [B]--dc23/eng/20230729
LC record available at https://lccn.loc.gov/2023035025

Printed in the United States of America

table of contents

About the author: When not writing, Dr. Virginia Loh-Hagan serves as the Director of the Asian Pacific Islander Desi American (APIDA) Center at San Diego State University. She is also the Co-Executive Director of The Asian American Education Project. She lives in San Diego with her very tall husband and very naughty dogs.

About the illustrator: Jeff Bane and his two business partners own a studio along the American River in Folsom, California, home of the 1849 Gold Rush. When Jeff's not sketching or illustrating for clients, he's either swimming or kayaking in the river to relax.

I was born in 1755. I was born in Austria. I was a **noble**.

I hated school. But I loved music.
I sang. I danced.

Do you like music?

I moved to France. I married the future king. This made peace. Austria and France became **allies**.

I became queen. I loved being a mother. I had four children. I also **adopted orphans**.

I helped poor people. I gave food. I gave money. I visited them.

13

I loved fancy things. I loved to have fun. I spent a lot of money.

What do you do for fun?

France was in **debt**. I was blamed. There were many **rumors**. People said bad things.

There was a **revolution**. People told me to flee. I fled with my family. We were jailed.

I died in 1793. But my **legacy** lives on. I was France's last queen.

What would you like to ask me?

1770

1750

Born
1755

Died
1793

1778

1850

glossary & index

glossary

adopted (uh-DAHP-tuhd) cared for another person's child as one's own

allies (AL-eyez) friends or supporters

debt (DET) the state of owing money

legacy (LEH-guh-see) anything passed down from a person in the past

noble (NOH-buhl) having royal blood

orphans (OR-fuhns) children without parents

revolution (re-vuh-LOO-shuhn) a war to end the rule of a government to start a new one

rumors (ROO-muhrz) stories that are not proven to be true

index